ALLISON SEARSON

Journey to the Authentic Me

Copyright © 2023 by Allison Searson

ISBN: 978-1-7376478-7-4

All rights reserved. No part of this publication may be reproduced, distributed, or transmitted in any form or by any means, including photocopying, recording, or other electronic or mechanical methods, without the prior written permission of the publisher, except certain other noncommercial uses permitted by copyright law. All quotes are cited within the content, reference by the author, or are unknown and are not being credited to the work of any contributing authors of this book.

Edited By Shawn Jackson

Published by One2Mpower Publishing LLC

www.one2mpower.com

INTRODUCTION

I was always the quiet one. The type of kid who would sit in the back of the class and not say anything unless I absolutely had to. I was known as the quiet, shy girl. I was so quiet, yet observant, that people used to ask me questions like "Do you talk?" or "You got an eye problem?" I never wanted to be in the forefront. I always preferred to be in the background, but God said, "Nah! Daughter, I'm calling you forward!" So, here I am sharing how God helped me conquer my battles with fear, the unknown, rejection, and double-mindedness. As my sister Alyssa told me, I'm slayin' these giants, so my kids won't have to.

Journey to the Authentic Me

ACKNOWLEDGMENTS

Shout out to God for pulling me out of my comfort zone with this one. My other books had more of a go-with-the-flow type of feel, but this one's different; it's weightier because people's lives and freedom are attached to it. God gets the glory out of this! Shout out to my amazing family for having my back no matter what and for always being there for me. A special shout out to my parents and my sister for always being a listening ear and always covering me in prayer. I also want to thank my Permission Room coaches, Jalisa Alston and Lexie McLamore, for hearing God and always declaring what thus says the Lord. God gave them the vision of this first before He gave it to me, and I'm so grateful they both heard God and were obedient. I also want to thank one of my pastors, Dr. Jackie Greene, for being obedient to God by starting Permission Room and for her authenticity. She always says, "Free people, free people," and she is

Journey to the Authentic Me

absolutely right! Her operating in her authentic self helped free me! She poured into us day after day, week after week, and I'm eternally grateful for that! Shout out to ALL of my Forward City family because they have all contributed to my growth and the woman I am today. Last, but not least, I also want to thank my amazing publisher, Robin Major-Oliphant, for making this process easy for me. A special thank you to ALL my supporters. You don't go unnoticed! I LOVE YOU ALL, and I thank God for each of you!

Love,

Allison

TABLE OF CONTENTS

Introduction iii

Acknowledgments v

CHAPTER 1: This Is Me 1

CHAPTER 2: Suppressed Memories Called Testimonies 5

CHAPTER 3: Feeling Lost 19

CHAPTER 4: Double-Mindedness 29

CHAPTER 5: Rejection and Perception 37

CHAPTER 6: Reception and Shame 45

CHAPTER 7: Fear and Doubt 55

CHAPTER 8: Belief and Consistency 65

CHAPTER 9: The Waiting (Patience) 75

CHAPTER 10: Purity 85

CHAPTER 11: Healing and Freedom 91

CHAPTER 12: Thriving Connections 99

CHAPTER 13: What's Next? 103

Journey to the Authentic Me

CHAPTER 1

THIS IS ME

Journey to the Authentic Me

Hi. My name is Allison. I'm twenty-nine years old, a native of South Carolina, and I love all things purple. I've taught second grade and am now teaching first grade. I sing and I write. I guess you could call me a small-town girl with big dreams. I dream of being free to minister, sing, and worship God freely, travel the world, and sign my own paychecks. A recent dream of mine was to own my own record company. I just have to put in the work and learn the ropes, e.g., all of the logistics of how to operate the machinery. I honestly never thought I would want to do this.

If you had asked nineteen-year-old me if twenty-nine-year-old me would be doing any of the things listed above, my answer would have been NO, *and* I'd think you were nuts! I was always very shy and quiet; talking just wasn't my thing. Don't get me wrong, if we were family or close friends, I'd talk, but if I didn't know you, you wouldn't hear a peep out of me. I was like this throughout school, and I'm still learning to break out of my shell even now. With the help of God, I'm still learning to break the spirit of "mute" because there's a lot God wants to do, but He can't if I remain silent.

It's a blessing to be alive because if the devil had it his way, I wouldn't be here. Before I was even born, he tried to

This Is Me

kill me. My mother was seeing a certain OBGYN for her checkups when she was carrying me, and he urged her to have an abortion because he said I could possibly have the sickle cell disease because she had the sickle cell trait and it would be unfair to bring me into the world only for me to go through such horrendous pain. Rather than listen to him, she listened to God and opted for a new physician. When she told me that story, right then and there, I knew I had a special call on my life for the enemy to try and take me out before I even got here, and he's been trying ever since. BUT the Word of God in Isaiah 54:17 KJV tells me, "No weapon that is formed against thee shall prosper; and every tongue that shall rise against thee in judgment thou shalt condemn. This is the heritage of the servants of the Lord, and their righteousness is of me, saith the Lord."

Although the weapons might form, they *won't* prosper because I'm covered. I'm covered by the blood of Jesus, and nothing can happen without His stamp and seal of approval.

Journey to the Authentic Me

CHAPTER 2
SUPPRESSED MEMORIES CALLED TESTIMONIES

A while back, God told me I really had NO idea of all that He kept me from. These included memories I have that I tried not to think about to the point where I eventually "forgot" about them. These are called suppressed memories. Suppressed memories are basically memories of things that have happened to you or things you've experienced you force yourself not to think about or forget that these experiences have even happened. God brought a few things to my mind that, against my will, He said I had to share. It's not my will, but Thine will be done, so I will be obedient and submit to the Father because my experiences can help free someone else.

I was in potential danger and didn't even realize it. When I was a little girl in elementary school, someone close to me would often pick me up from school whenever my parents or grandparents couldn't and take me to my grandparents' house. I hated riding with this person because he often smoked and reeked of it. However, on this particular day, I was riding with this individual when he seemed to be high, drunk, or a combination of both. When he picked me up, he told me my mom had gone out of town to Columbia with my grandparents, so essentially, no one would be there when we arrived. I heard what he said, but when we got to my grandparents' house, for some reason, I still rang the doorbell, and for some reason, this really agitated him. I remember him getting frustrated, and he said, "Didn't I just tell you they all went out of town?! Don't make me *rape* you." I remember looking astounded and murmuring, "Huh?"

I was very young at the time and didn't know what "rape" meant, but I knew it must've been something really bad. Once I got into the house, I remember going into my aunt's room and closing the door to do my homework. He went into the opposite part of the house and didn't come out for a while. I remember him peeking into the room to ask if I was okay. I said, "Uh huh," and went about trying to do my homework. After hearing my answer, he went back to whatever he was doing, and after a while, my mom and the rest of my family came back from out of town. I didn't say anything and went about it like normal, and he didn't say anything either.

I didn't understand the gravity of what could've happened to me. I need you to understand that **NOTHING happened,** and **I'M SO GRATEFUL!** I always wondered what exactly it was I did that would provoke him to make that type of threat toward me. I mean, all I did was ring the doorbell. I was so young, and I thought it must've been my fault, or I must've done something wrong for him to threaten me like that.

This is a memory I suppressed to the point that I had "forgotten" about it. God allowed it to resurface because I never dealt with it. I've only told my immediate family about the experience, but I told them many years after it happened. They asked why I didn't share it with them right when it happened, so they could've dealt with it right then and there, and my honest answer was, "I don't know." I don't know why I never told them or anyone in our family. I guess I was afraid no one would believe me, and he would get really mad at me and retaliate against me for telling. I guess it was all because of *fear*.

I don't think he remembers what he said to me. I don't think he even realizes he said it. I think he was really high, drunk, or a combination of both, and he wanted to evoke fear in me. As my mom and I talked deeper about it, we both came to the conclusion that it was all about control. God revealed to her that he wanted me to listen to him and be afraid of him. He wanted me to think he could harm me in some type of way if I didn't listen to what he said. Although he threatened me with rape, he wouldn't have actually done it. You know why? He couldn't do it to me because I was covered and still am covered! It was God that kept me, protected me, and covered me! God couldn't let that happen because it would have destroyed me, divided my family, and it would've destroyed that individual as well. But God! God blocked it, and I'm forever grateful! Thank You, Father, for protecting my innocence! I'm grateful this wasn't a part of my story, but my heart goes out to all the women, and even men, who have experienced and dealt with rape. I pray God would heal you of all traumas in Jesus' name. Amen.

> *Praise report on this individual: he's since put down the bottle, picked up the Bible, inquired about Jesus and Scripture, and we're praying he'll put down the cigarettes.*

This next thing I am about to share rocked my world and community. I always try to see the good in people, no matter what I may have heard. I always give people a clean slate, just like Jesus does. God brought me back to my first year of teaching in the 2018-2019 school year. I was very naïve and was still learning about people. A coworker of mine was often in need of a ride. Now that I think about it, this person had interesting and strange mannerisms I didn't pick up on at the time.

Now, being that it was my first year teaching and I was still learning the ropes, I was often at the school very late into the evenings; however, on this particular day, I was packed up and ready to leave the school early as soon as the last kid left my room. It was an afternoon in February, and I was headed to my car in the parking lot. The coworker I mentioned earlier was outside and was motioning toward me. I thought he was waving goodbye, so I said, "Have a great afternoon!" But instead, he was asking what direction I was headed and if I would mind giving him a ride. I was in between two opinions: part of me (my gut) felt like I should say no (which I later knew was the Holy Spirit's urging). The other part of me wanted to help him out and give him a ride since I often rode to my first-year induction classes with another coworker, but he wasn't like her.

I chose the latter and agreed to give him a ride. It was a typical ride. I played my music like I normally did, and he talked on his phone the entire way to what I assumed was his house. We arrived, and he offered me gas money. I refused and told him he was good. He got out and seemed in a hurry to get inside his house. I drove off and went on about my business. That was that, and it seemed pretty normal, right? WRONG! The next day shook up mine, my community, and my entire workspace's world!

The very next day, everybody in administration thought he had quit because he didn't show up to work and didn't call out sick, but boy, were they wrong. I remember us having an emergency staff meeting that afternoon (the end of the school day), and I wondered what it could have been about...It was about my coworker. After everyone was inside the library, our meeting room, our boss announced our fellow coworker had been arrested for *murder*. Yes, he was arrested for murder. In fact, he, along with everyone in the house I dropped him off at the day before! I remember sitting in my chair, feeling like the absolute wind was knocked out of me! People were gasping, panicking; we were all in utter shock! I know I didn't know him like that, but being arrested and doing something so horrendous was the farthest thing from my mind because he looked like he wouldn't hurt a fly.

I've seen stories like that on TV, but I never thought something like that could happen to me or my community.

Fear crept its way into my heart and mind because I was like, "I literally just gave that dude a ride the other day. And to the place where all those people were arrested." I didn't say anything, but you could see the fear, panic, and shock in my eyes and demeanor. I couldn't believe what I, and my other coworkers, were hearing. I was nervous to tell my family what had happened, but I told them anyway. I remember my dad telling me never to give a man a ride and to let them find their way to where they needed to go. Others also told me to respond with, "I'm not going that way," if the question was ever posed again in the future (it wasn't). I felt like I was being lectured for doing something wrong. I felt like I did something wrong by giving him a ride. Since I was the last one to give him a ride, my boss met with me to see how I was doing. I remember telling her I was just trying to help, and I would've given any of my coworkers a ride if they were in need of one. We later did a workshop as a whole school and talked about our feelings and our emotions from all that had happened. Needless to say, I wasn't the only one feeling afraid.

Suppressed Memories Called Testimonies

I was anxious, nervous, scared, and fearful. My mind immediately started playing scenarios in my head that could've happened but, thanks be to God, *didn't* happen. I started thinking things like, "He could've harmed me to take my car to get away…he could've done this; he could've done that." Like, man, I really could've been gone right now because you never know what the devil puts in people's heads and minds. But yet again, GOD KEPT ME, AND HE PROTECTED ME! I'M COVERED by His blood, and I'm oh so grateful!

I beat myself up a lot about that whole situation. I was like, "I have discernment, and I have the Holy Spirit, so how did I not know something was off about that dude? How did I not see this coming?" But then I remembered I *was* in between two opinions of what to do, and I *chose* the latter, although I felt at first I should've said no. This taught me to *always* go with my gut instincts/feelings called the "Holy Spirit" because He *won't* lead me wrong. He *won't* lead me astray. But I'm eternally grateful to God for keeping me. He's such a good, good Father!

The last suppressed memory that has also contributed to my fear(s) has to do with driving. Anybody who knows me knows I am *always* driving. Whether it is driving for my mom or grandma, or any other family member, I always seem to be driving (unless my dad is the one driving). In fact, I drive so much that one of my uncles teases me by calling me "Truck Driver." But this suppressed memory could have been the end of "Truck Driver" and my mom. But once again, God came through with His covering and protection!

On this particular day, my mom and I went to Columbia to pick up an order from The Home Depot. While we were there, we visited my uncle sometime between the afternoon and evening. I kept telling my mom I wanted to leave and be back on the road before it got dark because I didn't always see so well at night. She agreed, and we went on about our business. When we got there, we saw another uncle and aunt were over there as well, so we sat with them for a while. This was around the summertime when a lot of riots were breaking out in Columbia during the Black Lives Matter movement. We were sitting together watching the news, and the Holy Spirit urged me to say a prayer of protection over everyone before we departed. I'm glad I was obedient.

We left my uncle's house at a decent hour before it got dark and received a call from my dad asking for a meal from

Lizard's Thicket. The drive-thru line was ridiculously long, but we waited anyhow, and I remember saying, "I wanted to get home before it got dark." Nevertheless, we didn't get back on the road before dark. We got Dad's food, and Mom and I headed home. I was listening to music and concentrating on the road, and my mom was looking at her phone (she may have been doing a Bible plan, but I'm not sure). We were on 378 towards Sumter, and it was really dark because there were no streetlights on the highway and no other cars were on the road with us at that time.

I was going the speed limit (60 mph), and I remember my mom yelling and screaming because she saw deer approaching us. It all happened so quickly; I swerved to keep from hitting it, but a deer ran smack into my car on the driver's side. The run-in with the deer was so loud, I was so scared, and my car sounded really bad afterward! Mind you, we were two women, it was dark, and there was no one else there to assist us, so we figured we had to try to make it the rest of the way home (we still had about an hour to go). We prayed, and Mom calmed me down. I was more concerned about whether she was okay and wondered how badly my car was torn up. I understood the car could be replaced, but neither of us could.

My mind went back to earlier when God had me pray a prayer of protection. Who knows what would've happened to us had we not been obedient and had we not prayed! I'm so grateful for the Holy Spirit's urging, for us recognizing His voice, and for us being obedient. When I got home, I saw the damage wasn't all that bad, and it was mostly to my driver's headlight area. We got it fixed, the insurance company covered it, and that was that. But most importantly, *God covered us!*

These are testaments to God's love, goodness, faithfulness, covering, and protection. He's Jehovah Jireh, our provider; Jehovah Nissi, our banner and victory; Jehovah Shalom, our peace; Jehovah Rapha, our healer; Elohim, the Mighty One; and El Roi, the God that sees! I would not be here if it weren't for Jesus' blood being shed for me over two thousand years ago. None of us would be here if it weren't for His grace! I'm grateful and thankful to God for Him seeing fit to allow me to see another day, give me another chance to get it right with Him and pray, live out my purpose and calling for Him, and share my testimonies with

Suppressed Memories Called Testimonies

you all. I hope this charges you to remain strong in the faith, trust Abba, our Father, to protect and keep you, and know that it's Him, and *only* Him covering you!

Journey to the Authentic Me

CHAPTER 3
FEELING LOST

Journey to the Authentic Me

I've always been a "church girl." God and church were all I've ever known. In fact, I was a PGK (preacher's grandkid) and was raised up serving heavily in the church. From teaching Sunday School to presiding over youth services, singing in the choir leading worship, to serving as Sunday School superintendent and secretary, you name it, and I've pretty much done it. Church of God by Faith was all I knew because I grew up in the organization. I had been in it my whole life until something happened…my beloved granddaddy, who had also been my shepherd my whole life, got sick, and his assignments from church shifted. Let me backtrack, Granddaddy had been battling cancer, and I believe he suffered in silence for a long while before any of us knew what was happening.

Granddaddy devoted over forty years of his life to serving God and His people. He was one of the most genuine, kind-hearted, patient, compassionate, and selfless people I knew. Oh, and he was funny, too. There was never a dull moment! He *never* complained. Even when he wasn't feeling his best, he still didn't complain. The man never had a bad day. If he did, you'd never know about it because he wouldn't let anything rain on his parade. The only time I can recall I'd

Feeling Lost

ever seen him the slightest disappointed was when we were at an annual church convention and he received notice that his assignment was switching, and ultimately, we'd be moving churches. The original assignment was over an hour away, but the assignment which he took on was a little over thirty minutes from our city: Summerton. Honestly, none of us were thrilled about this location because it was literally in the middle of nowhere. No shopping mall in sight, and where would we go to eat afterward?! Nevertheless, he and our family took on the assignment, and that's who the church mostly consisted of, our family. Phillip, Brian Jr., Alyssa, and I held it down for the worship team Sunday after Sunday pouring our hearts out into worship of our Heavenly Father as if there were millions there. Granddaddy preached his heart out week after week, and all our relatives held it down and served in any capacity they could. I mean, we were faithful, faithful.

As time went on, Granddaddy got sicker and sicker and weaker and weaker. I knew he had lost weight drastically, but I guess I was oblivious to what was happening...or maybe I didn't want to accept it.

Surgery after surgery, and even the removal of a cancerous kidney, eventually led to Granddaddy's retirement from preaching. Like, what?! I didn't think that was possible. I always thought he'd just preach on and eventually be carried away to the pearly gates, just like Elijah the prophet. I remember it was suggested he be placed in hospice and how he had to sleep in a hospital bed instead of his own with Grandma, which broke my and everybody else's hearts. He eventually ended up in a nursing and rehabilitation center in Columbia around the same time Pastor Travis Greene announced the launch of Forward City Church. Because Granddaddy, my lifelong shepherd, was no longer pastoring, I was pretty much church hopping, feeling empty and lost. I loved where I came from, but a shift had taken place. I was growing sporadically spiritually and longed to be fed. I longed for *more*, and I wasn't getting that where I was.

I got wind of Forward City Church, and since Granddaddy was in Columbia, I suggested we check out the church and visit Granddaddy afterward. I remember it like it was yesterday. It was a Forward U service for the college students, and Da' T.R.U.T.H. was one of Pastor Travis' special

Feeling Lost

guests (Grandma wasn't with it LOL). Since we were first timers, we met Pastor Travis and Pastor Jackie. I remember Pastor Travis praying for us as he heard about what brought us there. It was genuine and heartfelt, and it was at that moment I *knew* I was home.

Even though I felt at home upon my first visit to Forward City, I was still church hopping because of wanting to please my family. I know, I know. You gotta go where you can grow, and I honestly don't know what I was thinking because I felt miserable any place else. Eventually, in March 2017, to be exact, I made the decision to make Forward City my home. After a few months of going there, my granddaddy popped this question on me, "When are you gonna get on that stage?" He was talking about the worship team. I had always been in some form of ministry in the church but preferred to be in the background. Whether it was on the choir or the praise team at my previous church, I always wanted to stay in the background...the girl who would be seen and not heard, if you will, and at the time, I was okay with that.

I joined the Sumter Life Group and made some wonderful connections. I even started some singing lessons with my then Life Group leader. I saw that Forward City was having auditions and keeping my granddaddy's question in mind (this was around October 2017, and by this time, Granddaddy had gone on to be with Jesus), I decided to go for it (I had not sought God about it). Lo and behold, I didn't make the cut for the second round of auditions and didn't take it well...I took it as rejection. Mind you, I was dealing with loss and grieving my sweet grandfather. I thought by auditioning, I would somehow make him proud by getting on that stage, but this was not what my Heavenly Father had for me at that time. I was in a different mental space than I am now. Although I loved my church and pastors, I felt angry, frustrated, confused, defeated, and rejected because, after all, isn't me being on that stage what Granddaddy saw? Although I felt this way, I kept my feelings hidden; I suffered in silence and cried about it all the time because I didn't think I was worthy or good enough...yeah, my thinking was all jacked up.

During this time, I was still in school (college), and I didn't know where my life was headed. I was studying education, not because I wanted to, but because I thought that was the only thing I could do. Don't get me wrong, I LOVE kids, and I always had the desire to do some type of work that would involve bettering children, but I didn't think teaching was my

Feeling Lost

jam. Around this time, I was a senior in college and would graduate in May of 2018. I remember my earlier college years when I so desperately wanted to be a pediatrician but was told by my then-academic counselor my scores "weren't high enough," so basically, my chances of getting into medical school were slim to none. *Sheesh* that put a damper on my already low self-esteem. I knew I couldn't be undecided in my major forever, so teaching it was. I eventually became okay with it, and now I realize it was all a part of God's plan for my life.

Around this same time, summer of 2017, I started writing. Before this, I remember being at a service my granddaddy was preaching, and after the service, a young man named Princeton asked if I wrote (at the time, I did not). He told me about a dream he had in which I was singing a song he'd never heard before and said I really helped him. I'm going to be completely and totally honest...I really thought he was nuts. I helped him? Bro, how? It was a dream. I wasn't even there! Me singing? Nah, I only did that if I was in the background (so sorry if you're reading this, but hey, the Lord was working in you, and you were right)! What I love about God is that He *always* confirms His word! A few months after this, my Life Group Leader asked me the same question that Princeton asked, "Do you write?" and I kid you not, that very night after Life Group, I wrote my very first song, "Urgency." It was originally titled "Messages from Heaven," and it wasn't complete at the time, but it was a start...a start to something beautiful I couldn't have ever imagined.

After losing my granddaddy, I was heartbroken and felt broken and empty. I had a void that could only be filled by my Heavenly Father, and while I was feeling lost and confused, little did I know my Daddy was pursuing and chasing after me. He started giving me specific times to meet with Him. I was praying a whole lot more, fasting more, journaling more, and writing more. In fact, a good bit of the songs from "Messages from Heaven" were birthed during this time, but at the time, I was like, "Okay, God. You and I are doing this. I'm writing like You said, now what do I do?" I had all these beautiful songs but didn't know what to do with them, so I waited. I waited three years, to be exact. "Urgency" was written in the summer of 2017, but it wasn't produced until November 2019 and released until January 31, 2020, in honor of my granddaddy's birthday. My pastor, Pastor Travis, declared 2020 the year of "Seek," seeking God. And boy, I tell you, 2020

Feeling Lost

was *definitely* that! I sought God daily and fasted a ton, and God birthed MORE songs, and He even birthed novels through me. It's really been a blessing.

During this time, whenever I felt lost, had no idea what was happening, and felt like I was floating or existing on Earth, I was reminded that God ordered my steps. I'm more than just existing. I'm not lost or aimlessly roaming the Earth. God has a plan for my life, and as long as I keep my ears to His mouth, stay in tune with Him, and stay in step with Him, I'll never be alone because He's with me. He's guiding me every step of the way. Even when I can't see it or feel it, He's working on my behalf, and I'm forever grateful.

Journey to the Authentic Me

CHAPTER 4

DOUBLE-MINDEDNESS

Journey to the Authentic Me

I'm always in my head, and it's a *huge* problem! I'm way too thinky. I overthink *everything!* If there was a poster child for over-thinkers, I'd definitely fit the bill! I'm my own worst enemy in this area of my life. It's actually ridiculous...it doesn't matter if it's the most complicated thing OR the simplest of things. You can bet either way, I'm gonna overthink it, and I honestly hate it! My mentality be like, "Well, if I do this, then that could happen. OR if I do that, then XYZ could possibly happen." It's absolute torture thinking of absolutely everything that could possibly go wrong instead of focusing on all the things that can and will go right, especially with obedience to God.

I remember years ago, sitting inside a bank waiting to be served, when I made eye contact with an older lady. I heard in my spirit something along the lines of "Be healed in Jesus' name." And boy, did I battle with myself in my mind (I'm shaking my head at the very thought of this). Half of me was like, "Yo, Allison, just go ahead and tell her. Ye ain't got nothin' to lose because she don't know you and you don't know her, but just say what God said." And then the other half of me was like, "Yo, she gone think you crazy forreal. What if she don't even believe in Jesus?" I mean, it was this, that, and the third happening in my thoughts based off a simple instruction, and by the time I had battled with myself, the opportunity was lost because my name was being called so that I could be served. I silently prayed for her in my mind, but that wasn't the instruction. The instruction was for me to tell her she was healed verbally. Then it hit: GUILT!

I felt guilty because I *knew* in my heart of hearts what I was supposed to do. But I freaked out, nearly gave myself a panic attack, reasoned myself out of saying what God told me to say, and then the opportunity was gone because I ran from it (I'm cringing at myself and shaking my head as I write this). I don't know what would've happened ...she could've been blessed by it. She could've been waiting for someone to confirm what she already knew was coming. Even if she didn't know Jesus, I could've used that as an opportunity to tell her about Him and how much He loves her. That ate at me for a long time; even while I was being serviced, I was thinking about it, and I eventually worked up the courage to tell her, only to find out she was gone. The guilt I felt was so weighty that I vowed to say and do whatever God told me to, no matter how uncomfortable it made me.

Unfortunately, I still had slipups...I mean, I'd go back and forth in my thoughts all day long if you'd let me (my parents and sister be so sick of me)! I know I'm not perfect, but good grief! Another occurrence happened while I was in church a couple of years ago. A young man was encountering the Holy Spirit for what I believe to be the first time, and I was instructed to go minister to him. At the time, I hadn't done much of that, especially to people I didn't know very well, and yet again, I was terrified out of my mind (ridiculous, I know). Yet again, I thought a silent prayer would suffice, but *no*. I had been disobedient yet again, even though I knew his heart was willing and open. I spent the remainder of that service feeling weighted, guilt, and begging pardon with God for not following His command. I. Was. Sorry.

The game changer for me was, and I'll never forget, a Sunday I was serving. It was towards the end of service, and people were ministering, pouring into one another, and praying for others. I remember falling to my knees and bowing before my Heavenly Father, the King of Kings. I felt whom I perceived to be my good sis SiQuena's hand on my back amongst several others who ministered to me. I'll never forget hearing these words: "Stop disqualifying yourself

Double-Mindedness

from the work the Lord has told you to do. It's time you stop telling God no and start telling Him yes!" That, that right there, was the breaker for me. I didn't want to disappoint God, I didn't want to go to hell for disobedience, and I didn't want others going there either. That day I *really* made up my mind I would do whatever the Lord said.

Although I'm a bit bolder and a little more confident, I'm still a work in progress. The enemy desires to have a playing field in my mind, and it's honestly a battle. The enemy has even fought me about how I view and think about myself. Y'all, I'm twenty-nine years old, and I'm just now liking and loving me…tis a shame, I know, I know. Growing up, I used to compare myself, especially to my cousins, because they were thinner than me. I've always been on the heavier and chunkier side, always been shy, always been awkward with glasses, and lacked confidence. I did *not* like myself or the way I looked. I used to see young pretty girls and think, "Why can't I be like them?" or "Why don't I look like them?" See, things may look well on the outside, but I had no clue what they were going through on the inside. The grass always looks greener on the other side, but you have no idea what battles and demons people are battling. Just because everything looks good doesn't mean it's really good! I had my self-esteem issues going on, so I didn't think about stuff like this then. I didn't know I was and am beautiful, perfectly, fearfully, and wonderfully made by my Daddy. I didn't know I was *already* worth it, and if I didn't like my weight or how I looked, to change it. I'm beautiful now, and I was beautiful then. *Periodt.*

Writing this has been a battle because the enemy knows what this will accomplish, so he's doing everything in his power to keep me foggy and distracted, but *it won't work!* You see, I was supposed to write this over three years ago when my mentors first told me to, but I put it off because it made me uncomfortable, and I shed lots of tears. Thank God for His grace and mercy! He reminded me about that which I had started three years ago and charged me to get it done THIS year! I prayed and even battled with myself about what was to be shared because of fear of being out there. The reality is, as my pastors always say, "Free people, free people." I have no idea who this story is supposed to touch. But *I do know* it will accomplish all it's supposed to accomplish and reach who it's supposed to reach, which is mind-boggling to me.

Double-Mindedness

I wish I could tell you I've mastered my thoughts. I wish I could tell you I've mastered being too thinky and overthinking. It's honestly still a battle and work in progress, but I CAN tell you I ain't nowhere near where I was before (praise the Lord for progress)!

It's like I have high highs or either low lows. Sometimes I'm up, sometimes I'm down, or somewhere in the middle especially relating to the promises of God. Sometimes I'm on cloud nine and be like, "God and I are doing this!" And other times, I'm a hot weepy, mopey mess like, "God, when are you gonna come through for me?" Yes, that, my friends is double-mindedness, and the Bible puts it like this in James 1:6-8 NKJV "6 But let him ask in faith, with no doubting, for the one who doubts is like a wave of the sea that is driven and tossed by the wind. 7 For that person must not suppose that he will receive anything from the Lord; 8 he is a double-minded man, unstable in all his ways." *Sheesh! Yikes*, but that's Bible!

I don't want to go back and forth with myself in my thoughts; in fact, *I hate it!* It causes so much unnecessary stress, frustration, and pain, not to mention headaches, and the worst part is it's self-inflicted. I constantly do this to myself, and I'm tired of this cycle. That's exactly what it is: a cycle, and it's time to BREAK THE CYCLE! I declare no more going back and forth in my thoughts, no more talking myself out of what God has spoken and declared over me, and no more not doing what God says for me to do! I WILL be sound in my thoughts and decisions because 2 Timothy 1:7 tells me God has already given me a SOUND MIND! Romans 12:2 NKJV also tells us to "not be conformed to this world, but be transformed by the renewal of your mind, that by testing you may discern what is the will of God, what is good, pleasing, and perfect."

I'm not 100% where I want to be yet, *but* I am getting better! Whenever I feel bombarded by my thoughts, I'm reminded to quote scripture. Hebrews 4:12 NKJV tells us, "For the word of God is living and active, sharper than any two-edged sword, piercing to the division of soul and spirit, of joints and marrow, and discerning the thoughts and intentions of the heart." God cuts down the stronghold of my thoughts, and it will get better with each day that passes.

CHAPTER 5
REJECTION AND PERCEPTION

Journey to the Authentic Me

I've always been sweet, quiet, awkward, quirky, and shy (heavy on the shy). I was the type of girl that whenever I entered a room, you probably wouldn't even know I was there unless you saw me with your own eyes because I was just that quiet. I was the speak only when spoken to kind of girl, unless we were family, or I knew you knew you. I was heavily introverted, and most people thought and viewed me as weird and judged me. I've been accused of thinking I'm all that, thinking I'm better than everyone else, thought I had it all together, some people thought I didn't know how to talk, you name it, and the list goes on and on. People used to make fun of me and tease me because I was chunky and on the heavier side. In my younger elementary school years, this used to really bother me, and the only way I thought I could stop it was to become like them: mean. Yep, I became a bully, and *I hated it*. That was the only way I thought I could get them to stop bothering me, but I was *wrong!* My breaking point was when I realized I had said something really mean and called my cousin, who was like my best friend, a mean name because I didn't get my way in a game. When I saw the hurt look in her eyes and the tears streaming down her face, I realized I was wrong, really wrong, and had to make a change. I apologized to her, and I made a promise to myself I would never make others feel the way some jerks made me feel. So, I went back to not saying anything and just taking the verbal abuse.

Around fourth and fifth grade and beyond, was when things got worse. There was this "popular" group of girls in my class who, at the time, thought they ran things. They. Were. *Mean*. But they were as pretty as can be, and I so desperately wanted them to like me, but they didn't. They made fun of my clothes, called me names, and I remember being terrified of going to the girls' restroom because one of them had threatened to beat me up. Honestly, this was all really stupid and ridiculous. I never told my teachers what was happening, and I ain't even tell my parents till maybe a few years later…the trauma. Because of a few idiotic girls, I took on this mentality that, somehow, I must be unlikeable. Surely there must be something wrong with me to have to suffer in this way. Surely I'd done something for them to absolutely dislike and hate me. That's what I felt, and that's what I believed for a long, long time.

In my teenage years and even in my early adult years, I always worried about how people perceived me. I always worried about what people thought about me and how they viewed me. I based my worth off peoples' opinions of me, and I so desperately wanted the approval of man that I didn't even realize I already had the approval of God, which means so much more! I wanted people to like me. I honestly just wanted friends, but I wasn't looking in the right places. The people I so desperately wanted to be friends with rejected me, one of them being my cousin (it really be your own people). At the time, I didn't see it as God's protection because I couldn't be unequally yoked (2 Corinthians 6:14). Amos 3:3 says, "Two can't walk together unless they agree," but at the time, I wasn't seeing or hearing this. I just saw it as nobody liked me, I was unlikeable, and something was wrong with me. But here's the kicker...I REJECTED ME.

God revealed to me it was I who rejected me. *I didn't like myself.* I didn't love myself. It was me that had the issues with me. I never felt pretty or good enough, especially when every guy (and it's literally only a few) I ever liked never seemed to have me to think about, so now I'm un-dateable and not worthy of love or being loved by a male. Sometimes I felt invisible. I felt unvalued and that folks just didn't see my worth. I know my worth and value don't come from people, it comes from God, but sometimes I'm like, "Don't they know I can do this or that? Can't they see this in me? Don't they know I can potentially make them happy?" This junk used to hurt so bad. I was good enough to be the cheerleader and supporter but not the lover. Or I was cool enough to talk to whenever he'd need a pep talk or some encouragement but was too lame to date or kick it with. Only good enough to be the homie, but not someone you'd actually want to be in a relationship with. I used to wonder what guys saw whenever they looked at me...maybe they saw an angel with a sword guarding me like the angel guarded the Garden of Eden to keep Adam and Eve out when they messed everything up for all of humanity. These were the thoughts that flooded my mind all the time to the point where I didn't realize God was just keeping me hidden until He saw fit to send the RIGHT one.

Y'all, I was even bullied in my very first workplace (shaking my head) about stuff like this. I got called gay because I'd never dated anyone and wasn't seeking any of the guys I worked with as a boyfriend. Oh, I can't forget the famous, "It's because your granddaddy is a preacher," when I was asked my views about premarital sex or anything mentioned in the Bible (*wait until you're married* was my answer and because my grandfather was a preacher they thought that was the only reason I was saying that, shaking my head again). I suffered from really bad acne at that time, and my then manager spread that I had a hickey on my neck to my other coworkers (it was NOT a hickey; I repeat, it was NOT a hickey). When I heard what she said, I nearly had a meltdown on the job. Like, *who* gets bullied for doing all they can to try to live holy and right?! Scripture tells us "All who want to live a godly life in Christ Jesus will be persecuted" (2 Timothy 3:12). Jesus Christ Himself went through persecution for being holy, so what made me think I wouldn't for trying to be like Him? Although she embarrassed me in front of many, I pulled her aside to address her and let her know how uncomfortable she'd made me. She apologized, but throughout the rest of my time working there with her, I could tell she wasn't too fond of me. I wasn't fond of her after that, but I never showed it. I kept treating her with respect and dignity, no matter how she treated me.

Back to the point of me not liking me: I didn't like me, so how in the world could I expect others to like me? I didn't love me, so how could I expect others to? *Crazy*, right?! The crazy thing is, I didn't even realize this was happening; I had no idea how much hatred I had for myself.

On the outside, looking in, you'd think I was the happiest person ever. I always kept a smile on my face no matter what (I still do). But on the inside was a different story. I was depressed...just sad for no reason at all. I was wearing a mask. It was all a façade. I'm not even gonna lie or pretend like I didn't have suicidal thoughts. Sometimes I thought the world would be much better without me, but now I know THIS IS A LIE from the pits of hell! Just goes to show that looks can be deceiving, and the grass ain't always greener on the other side. Thank God for a praying and discerning mama and for me not doing anything crazy to myself! Shout out to God for sending people (angels) to cover me when I didn't even know I needed covering! This is all a testament to our great and wonderful God, and prayerfully my testimony can help to free someone else.

I'm grateful for my story, but I'm even more grateful God showed me how to love me. I'm grateful He's changed my perception of me and has allowed me to see me as He sees me: fearfully and wonderfully made (Psalm 139:14). He says I'm perfect and worth it, and He says the same for you too, beloved.

Journey to the Authentic Me

CHAPTER 6
RECEPTION AND SHAME

Journey to the Authentic Me

I didn't like myself. *Yikes,* a disturbing and sad truth. It's really, and I mean extremely hard to believe others like you when you don't even like you. I honestly didn't love myself, and there were thoughts that people and the world would be better off without me. I was literally ashamed of myself because I thought something was wrong with me, but you'd never know that when you saw me *unless* you saw (through) me. Wow, I was really ashamed to be me! That's mind-boggling (Thank God for deliverance in my thinking)! Don't get me wrong; I wasn't out here running the streets or acting wild or crazy. I lived in a shell (and still do, but we're breaking out of it, amen), very much a homebody (and still am).

I never really understood the root of all of this until recently. I was invited to a friend's house for a night of worship, which turned into a night of healing, restoration, and freedom. A lot of my thoughts and feelings were brought up from my childhood. Not that I had a bad childhood or anything because I didn't, but through words that were spoken through certain people that I started to believe were true. I now know to reject everything said contrary to the Word of God and to *only* accept what God says about me. But back then, I didn't realize this. So, I thought if so-and-so said or thought this about me, then surely it must be true (*wrong*). I know this now, but I didn't know this then. I didn't know how to fight against word curses sent from the enemy. I know it sounds really stupid, but I thought what people thought of me was that, and there wasn't any changing it, which made me feel really bad and ashamed to be me.

Several instances come to my mind as I try to articulate the grip of people's approval and how much it had me in a chokehold. My hair is one of them. Growing up, my mom would do and style my hair, and when I started going to a beautician, for the most part, she picked the style too, and then she started letting me pick my own styles. I had thick, long hair, and it was a lot to manage. I remember being a youngin' and getting what I called "burning stuff" (a relaxer to chemically straighten my hair) put in my hair. It didn't do too well for me, though, and damaged my hair. So, we went back to the basics: back to natural hair with a press and curl, and then I was able to start choosing my styles. I'd mostly stick to the basics, nothing too crazy, but when I got older, I wanted to venture out more.

The first time I'd ever had any color put in my hair was my freshman year of high school. It wasn't a permanent color; it was a burgundy rinse that would do exactly what it's called: rinse out after a couple of washes. I eventually went back to relaxers too. Fast forward to my college years, and I did what was called the "big chop," where I chopped off all my relaxed hair to return my hair to its natural state, and boy, were some of my folks upset because I had long hair, but it was thin and unhealthy, and *really* unhealthy at that. But because it was long, some relatives asked, "Why would you cut all of your pretty, long hair?" They assumed I must've been going through some mental crisis. And these were folks who were close to me! As it grew, I put it in a lot of protective styles, whether it was crotchets, two-strand twists with added hair, or box braids, and whenever I'd get weave added, I could almost always count on a relative to say, "You cut off all your pretty long hair only to add weave in it?!" Oh, and don't let it be a colorful weave at that!

I remember wanting to try something crazy and out of the box: pink hair for box braids. I had never done anything like this and was so excited to try it! Shout out to my stylist, Capitola, for always being on board with my crazy ideas LOL! Anyway, I got the pink braids put in, and I got lots of stares...a random person I happened to be standing behind in line

Reception and Shame

turned around and made fun of me to her friend. That hurt a little bit, but it really be your own people. Don't get me wrong, some of my folks were all for it because they're artsy, creative, and like to try different things too, but the negativity outweighed the positivity in my case. I remember going to the home of my older and seasoned relatives, and the first thing out of one of their mouths was, "What is that you got in your hair? I *don't* like that!" Heavy on the don't and "What's wrong with just having black hair?" At that time, I was still trying to build my confidence, but this person kept expressing their disproval of it, and for some reason, it really meant a lot to me what they thought, so I took the braids down shortly afterward, feeling defeated and ashamed that I even went for it. It's crazy how other people's reactions or thoughts on something can have a major effect and change your perspective. You could love something one moment, talk with others about it, and then hate it the next.

I eventually got tired of the fro and protective styles all the time and had a dream that I loc'd my hair (my stylist had already seen this in the Spirit, but I didn't think I would do it until I, too, saw it in the Spirit LOL). So, lo and behold, I loc'd my hair, and when my locs started to mature, yep, you guessed it: I added color! Blonde, orange, and red to the tips of my locs, and eventually blue and purple. I absolutely *loved* it! I got lots of compliments, too, along with negative commentary from the same closed-minded people. But this time around, I didn't care what others thought. As long as I was happy, flourishing and thriving that was all that mattered to me. But I wish I could say the same when it came to my clothes.

If you were to see me today, you may think I'm a fashionista or have some swag LOL, but it wasn't always this way. I would very much dress like a senior citizen (I might be over exaggerating just a little, but you get the point) in my high school and college days, and it's mostly because I would settle for familiarity and not explore what my style really was. Because I put myself in a box, I guess it was expected I'd stay there by some, but my fashion-forward auntie has always been an inspiration for me, and she's very encouraging; others, not so much.

On this journey of liking and loving myself, self-love if you will, I have charged myself to take more selfies and even post some of them. I cringe at the thought of this, but not as much as I used to because I don't like to be the center of

Reception and Shame

attention; I don't like a lot of attention on me and would very much like to hide. One of my dear aunties charged me with stating positive affirmations over myself while looking in the mirror, and although it felt awkward and weird at first, it was vital that I do it. I even have an album of pictures on my phone titled "I Love Me." Not because I'm self-conceited or anything, but because now those three words are true. I really do love me now (here come the waterworks)!

Anywho, back to clothing. I'm now coming into my own and finding/figuring out what I like and what looks and feels good on me. I was gearing up for my cousin's wedding and trying to figure out what I'd even wear. Everything in my closet displeased me, which gave me an excuse to buy something new LOL. I mean, he was starting a new journey, so why not! It made perfect sense in my head. I found this beautiful green floral dress with a sweetheart neckline and puffy sleeves that came right to the knees. I got it from Shein. It looked beautiful on the model, but it was even more stunning when I saw it in person. I was initially skeptical because of the length, but I'm a short person, and it worked perfectly for me LOL. The sleeves were off the shoulder, and I loved the dress. I paired it with some fluffy socks, fresh white forces, and my mint-colored Minnie Mouse Loungefly backpack. Because we were still in COVID times, I wore a pink lace face mask with it. I looked and felt like a princess, so I had to get my good sis Alyssa to take some pics! I posted them on Facebook and Instagram and received lots of compliments, and others wanted the link so they could purchase the dress. I was on cloud nine, and then here came the negatives, "My have you changed," "I see you got all your back and shoulders out," "That's not the way to get attention," and "That's not the way to try to get a man to look at you," to name a few.

I was flabbergasted! Couldn't they see how happy I was? Didn't they know how long it took me to get to this place?! *Why did they assume I was looking for attention from a man?* Didn't they know I hated attention being on me and only posted the pics because I rarely did that, and I just so happened to feel cute that day? Didn't they know, and didn't they care? The worst thing was some of the comments weren't said directly to me...some were said to other relatives and then relayed the messages to me. What is your purpose in relaying said messages? What joy do you get out of this? The second worst thing was I started to rethink my

Reception and Shame

choices. Maybe I was showing too much (even though I wasn't showing anything at all), maybe it was too short (even though it came to my knees), was I really seeking attention (100% was not), and maybe I shouldn't wear something like this again, or I should try to be more modest (So dress like a nun?). I had to shove all these comments and thoughts out of my mind because, honestly, I wasn't doing anything wrong or out of character, and if the Holy Spirit didn't convict me, neither would I.

Don't even get me started on wearing makeup! Your girl knows *nothing* about how to do makeup, BUT I do think it's beautiful and a great way to enhance your already beautiful self. So far, I've had three professional photo shoots, two involving makeup. The first time I was gearing up to release my then-third single, "Talk Faith," and I wanted a fierce look for the cover. I didn't tell many people I was doing this because I already knew what their response would be, and honestly, I wasn't tryna hear any of it. A short time passed, and I got the pictures back and was again in love. Again, it was the same ones, plus some that had something to say: "You have on way too much makeup," "That's ungodly," and the list goes on and on. At that point, I was like, "Bro, what?!"

and started voicing how I felt. I stated how I'd never done anything like this prior, and it was a really great and fun experience. I basically told them I liked it and was happy, and that's all that mattered. By the next shoot for my twenty-eighth birthday, they learned to keep their commentary to themselves LOL.

The moral of the story is this: as long as you're pleasing the Father, that is all that matters. If you're not doing anything wrong, there's NO need for others' unsolicited thoughts, feelings, and opinions to make you feel bad or ashamed, especially because *you're not doing anything wrong!* Again, as long as God is pleased and you're happy, that's all that matters! If the Holy Spirit doesn't convict you, neither should you. *Love yourself* and do the things that make you happy! Live for God first, and live for you too. This is a lesson I had to learn and am still learning; I hope this really helps you! *I love you,* and most importantly, Jesus does too!

CHAPTER 7
FEAR AND DOUBT

Journey to the Authentic Me

For the longest time, fear has had a horrendous grip on me. I've allowed fear to cripple me for way too long. I was the biggest scaredy cat you'd ever meet. From Halloween masks to trying something new to voicing my opinion and telling how I really felt, you name it, and I was either scared of it, scared to do it, or a combination of both.

Growing up, my family and I never celebrated Halloween because in the church I was always taught that's the "devil's day" (He doesn't have a day, amen! The only day he gets is when he gets thrown into the eternal lake of fire in hell. *Periodt*). I was already terrified of Halloween because of the costumes and masks (I had a weird phobia), so hearing that made things ten times worse. We called it "Hallelujah Night" and went to church for praise and worship unto God, and they'd give us candy there (same concept, no?). My uncles were like my older brothers, and they liked to tease, trick, and scare me and my cousins. I remember Uncle Zo having this gorilla mask. I…was… *terrified* of that thing! Whenever he'd put it on, I knew it was him underneath it, but somehow there was still a disconnect in my mind (before you judge me, keep in mind that I was a youngin' LOL). I remember being outside with my cousin and some of his friends from our

Fear and Doubt

grandparents' neighborhood. I did something (can't remember what it was) one of my aunties didn't like, and my punishment...you guessed it...was her putting on that gorilla Halloween mask and chasing me around outside (she was *wrong* for that LOL). I...looked...like...a...fool! A fool, I tell you, a fool! I was hollering and screaming and crying, and my cousin and his friends were laughing. I was *embarrassed* and nearly had a panic attack. So, I decided to do something.

I decided to purchase my very own Halloween mask in hopes of ending my fear and phobia. This was hard because I nearly panicked walking by any of that stuff in the stores (I had a really big problem y'all). Lo and behold, I bought one from my local Dollar Tree, got it home, left it in the bag, and threw it in the top of my closet so I didn't have to see it. Then...I was terrified to go in my closet (I'm shaking my head at myself). With time and prayer of asking God to take that fear from me, I eventually overcame this fear that had a stronghold on me for so long. Now it's still not my thing (if it's your thing and you like it, do you boo), but I'm not shaking in my boots whenever this holiday approaches or takes place. I laugh now because it's funny when I reminisce, but it wasn't funny then. Now, now, you may think this is something trivial...but how about the fear of public speaking and rejection?

I was the type of girl that wouldn't say anything unless spoken to. If we were in church and you gave me a microphone, I'd give it right back to you as quickly as you gave it to me because I wasn't having it. I was the sit back and relax kind of girl. The girl that would rather be seen and not heard in the background. I was the girl that would cheer you on and support your dreams but never voice mine. I was the girl that would never voice her thoughts, feelings, or opinions because I didn't think it mattered. I was the girl who would have a song to sing and not sing it because I. Was. Scared. I was afraid...I was afraid of how people viewed me and how they'd receive me. So, I went on like this throughout school until I got to college.

I remember being in my very first public speaking class ever called Communications 101. I *hated* it because it took me out of my comfort zone. I was always under the time limit for my speeches, and any time I'd have to give a speech, I didn't want to be first or last because I'd nearly have a panic attack. My hands would get really shaky, my heart would always seem like it was beating out of my chest, and I knew

Fear and Doubt

the folks in my class could hear the quiver and shakiness of my voice. I was a hot mess, but my instructor was always positive and encouraging. It was also around this time that I learned I could be good at writing. In college, you write paper after paper, and some of them are lengthy. I remember taking my first English course and getting my paper back, and seeing all the positive comments from my instructor. She told me, "Allison, you're a really good writer. You have a lot to say, and you do it well." I remember thinking, "Me? I have a lot to say? Could I really be a good writer?" And the answer is yes.

I did (do) have a lot to say. I just didn't use my words. I wouldn't voice it out of fear. During this time, I started writing a whole lot more (this was around the time when my dear granddaddy went to be with Jesus). I started journaling and writing my thoughts, prayers, and then songs and poems were being birthed through me. I started practicing my speeches and eventually got less nervous (don't get me wrong, I was still nervous, but it wasn't nearly as bad as before). But then I completed that course and wasn't required to take another one like it. Back to my shell I went.

Journey to the Authentic Me

I remember being in church, and the Holy Spirit wanted me to minister to a young man. I was *terrified* to do it and ended up saying a prayer for him in my head. Then I heard, "It's life or death," and then came my old friend guilt again! From that day forward, I vowed never to let fear get in the way of what God wants to do through me again.

Back to songs and poetry...at the time, it all felt like a dream because I was like, "Okay, God. You gave this to me, but what do I do with it?" I couldn't see past where I was. I couldn't see it coming to fruition. Before Granddaddy passed, I remember him saying, "You and Alyssa could be like a Mary Mary." Again, I didn't see it then, but Granddaddy was right. Fast forward five years later, and your girl has a whole album, four singles, and two novels (third one will be released shortly after this) out! *Crazy,* isn't it?! Oh, and Alyssa is my bestie, for sure! She's the dopest of the dope! Crazy anointed, gifted, talented, and lethal with a camera. I don't know what we'll do in ministry together, but I know the Father has us.

So, your girl started working her way out of fear of ministering and talking to people. One of the gifts God has given me is discernment, and no matter how others try to

Fear and Doubt

make me feel, I *do* hear Him well. I may have messed up a few times along the way, but when I hear Him, *I hear Him*. There were a few instances in which those I was instructed to give a word to didn't adhere to or receive it well. One instance, in particular, is ringing really loudly in my ears. A girl I knew was in a relationship that God didn't want her to be in. I remember God speaking to me and telling me I had to be the one to tell her. The first time He said it, I tried to shake it off because it made me uncomfortable. I wasn't tryna be the one to tell her about her relationship. So, the first time I didn't. But the second time God spoke, I had no choice but to move, and He already told me how it was going to go, and it didn't end well.

I didn't have her telephone number, so I inboxed her on Facebook instead and wrote what God placed on my heart to share with her there. She didn't like it, nor did she receive it; she told me she hears God for herself, and He didn't tell her she needed to end her relationship. She called me spiritually immature for reaching out to her through Facebook. And that's not all. She eventually stopped talking to me altogether and blocked me. I left this situation feeling really defeated. Part of me was like, "Okay, God, I did what You said...now what?" And the other part of me began to question if that was what God really wanted me to do. I started to doubt myself and my ability to hear Him clearly because of the end result. I wanted it to be all sunshine and rainbows, when in reality, God had already told me she wasn't going to be receptive. This wasn't my first case of someone getting upset with me because I was being obedient (and I know it won't be the last); I had done what God said.

I've had some friends and even some family members get upset with me whenever I tell them what the Lord said concerning them. Some even got argumentative, but I had to learn to let it go and shake the dust off my feet after I had done what was required of me. If they received it, fine. If not, it's still fine. I had to learn it wasn't me they weren't receiving; it was God. It was God they were rejecting and getting upset with. I just happened to be the messenger. Jesus' own people didn't receive Him. Mark 6:4 NIV says, "Jesus said to them, 'A prophet is not without honor except in his own town, among his relatives and in his own home.'"

I was like, man going through all of this, I should've just stayed quiet. *Wrong!* That's what the enemy would want, but I'm taking the muzzle off! I can't remain in fear, I can't doubt what the Father spoke, and I can't stay quiet because God

Fear and Doubt

has been way too good, merciful, and kind, and there's a lot He desires to do and accomplish through me. I'm grateful to be His chosen vessel.

Journey to the Authentic Me

CHAPTER 8
BELIEF AND CONSISTENCY

I'm the girl that will celebrate others in a heartbeat. If you have good news, something went well for you, or if you were just in a great mood, I'm your girl. You can bet I'm going to celebrate you and celebrate with you. Oh, and let you not receive a word from the Lord or a prophecy because I'm going to celebrate you the loudest. The moral of the story is if we're family, if we're friends, or even if I know of you, you can bet your last I'm going to be your proudest and loudest cheerleader. Honestly, I'm just an all-around encourager to many, and I encouraged others when I needed it most for myself. But here's where things get interesting...here's the thing...I'll encourage you ALL day long, and I'll celebrate with and for you *all* day long, and I'll even believe God with and for you *all* day long, but the kicker is when it comes to me...I don't do it for myself.

I know, I know...you might be saying, "Now, Allison. Girl, what's wrong with you?! Why don't you celebrate you?!" And honestly, I. Don't. Know. Philippians 2:3-4 says, "Do nothing out of selfish ambition or vain conceit. Rather, in humility, value others above yourselves, not looking for your own interests but each of you to the interests of others." I definitely take that to heart! I'm not one who likes the limelight, and I feel really awkward when the attention is on me, so if I can thwart attention off me to someone else, you can bet 1000% I'm going to do that! Wanting to be seen but not wanting to be seen at the same time...weird, right?! Yep, weird is me.

I see for others...that's one of the many gifts that God has given me, and I'm truly grateful. I understand that because I see for others, some things I am required to share with them while other things are seen for me to pray for them. I also understand not everything will be sunshine and rainbows. Sometimes, tough talks have to be had, and sometimes I'm required to give hard or difficult words from the Lord that the recipient does not want to hear or may not want to receive, so I'm reluctant to give it, but I still do it. Now the happy words, I'll give in a heartbeat. I'll hype you up, rejoice with you, celebrate with you, and believe God for you! But once again, I won't do that for myself.

God checked me. He said, "You believe and see for others, but you don't see and believe for yourself. Have I not spoken My word over you? Have I not fully equipped you? Have I not shown you what you need to do for what is to come? If you have to see it to believe it, you're late! You must see it *before* you see it! Allison, I'm not a man that I would lie to you. You can trust Me. You can believe Me. My word is true. Don't you know Me? Haven't I already revealed Myself to you? It's going to happen for you. In fact, it IS happening for you. Things are turning around for you, BUT it's according to your faith. Get your faith up there, girl!" He literally had to drill that in my head until I got it until it clicked for me because *He's the same God!* The same God that did it for my bestie, the same God that did it for my homie, the same God that did it for my family is the *same God* that will and IS doing it for me (here come the waterworks)!

Faith without works is *dead* (James 2:26). You'll work towards what you believe, and I had to learn that. My actions and demeanor needed to line up with what God was and is showing me. Never cocky with it, but bold with it. I understood I was created for more than what I was seeing at the moment. It was like a paradigm shift. I was no longer just floating or existing. As I often say, I was thriving and truly living! I had to learn the hard way not to share my visions and dreams with everybody. I'd get so excited that I'd share with others prematurely, only to get knocked down shortly afterward because they didn't see or it hadn't been done in our family before. I realize that although they may have

Belief and Consistency

meant well, they were speaking out of fear, and I was trying to overcome fear and walk boldly in faith. I had to learn when and what to share and what not to share. God ain't give it to everybody; He gave it to me, so of course, they may not see it.

For example, in the summer of 2019, God instructed me to stop playing and purchase my passport because I would need it for where He's taking me. I told very few what I was doing and told the rest after I had already received it in the mail. It's currently 2023, and I've only used it once, but I know what God said. I remember a certain relative saying, "Why would you spend all that money and purchase a passport only to never use it?" Mind you I was one of the first to purchase one in my family. The enemy tried to play this comment in my head over and over again because I had already been dealing with doubt. *But God!* I remembered what God said! He said I needed to get my passport because I WILL be free to minister and travel. I didn't owe NOBODY any explanation for doing what God said. God and I have history; we got a track record, and I *know* He's gonna make good on His promise. He's gonna do what He said, and everything He spoke over me is *gonna be mine!* I just gotta be consistent.

Journey to the Authentic Me

I'm the type of girl that'll start something and then stop almost as soon as I start it. This story...my story...I started writing it three years ago when I was instructed, but because it brought on so many emotions and made me uncomfortable, I put it off until God literally made me pick it back up again. I guess you can say I avoid difficult tasks (*and do*). I have self-diagnosed myself with *Attention Deficit Disorder* because your girl gets distracted easily. The slightest thing can get me off task and lose focus, mainly social media, but also the most random thoughts that come across my mind. When I say random, I mean the most random thing, and then I find myself laughing at something that's really stupid for the next thirty minutes to an hour and get sidetracked with what I was originally doing. Even people are my distractions. I can be doing something or starting something and then get a random text or call from someone I haven't heard from in 5,000 years (I'm so dramatic LOL). Or get this, the ones closest to me can even be a distraction too. Like because I still live at home with my little sister and the parentals, they'll barge into my room (being dramatic again), and then I'll get unfocused again. I'm like Doug from the

Disney movie "Up" whenever a squirrel would run by him …easily distracted. *But I shall regain focus…Amen!*

Honestly, most of the time, I stop doing something because I didn't get the result(s) I thought I'd get, it didn't go how I thought it would, or it didn't look like how I thought it should, so I stopped. There were countless times I wanted to give up on singing and songwriting because I was trying to get my music out there and get folks to hear me. I've reached out to numerous radio stations, local and global, and have been told "no" or given no response at all…ignored, if you will. It's hard out here in these musical streets, and I don't do a good job of promoting my stuff because I don't want to be an annoyance to your timeline, and it feels really weird putting myself out there (one of the reasons I didn't want to write this). But because I have books and music out there, people just assume I'm stacking in racks of money, and that's not the case. It takes money to make money, and some of the ones closest to me constantly remind me I'm putting out more than I'm pulling in, which is quite discouraging to have that constant reminder. But I keep going…I've got to because this is *bigger* than me! And it's honestly not about the money…it's about evoking change. If I can help someone else, encourage them, or help them get through what I've been through, that's enough for me. I just want to walk out my calling and God-given purpose on this here Earth. I didn't give myself these dreams... *God did!* And He didn't make no quitter!

So yes, God's coming heavy for belief and consistency in my life. He's calling me to finish what's been started and to never quit or give up because I may not be able to see it all yet. He's calling me to be consistent in *every* area, *every* aspect of my life: my time with Him, my diet, my routine, *everything*. It's like working out and eating right. If you keep at it, eventually you'll see the results you're looking for and expecting, and boy, have I started and stopped with my fitness journey several times...too many to count, but if I want to lose weight, I have to be consistent and put in the work for it! You'll work for what you want, and I want *everything* God has for me; I want everything He's promised me, so I have to be consistent. I've got accountability partners, and most importantly, God is holding me accountable for everything He's instructed me to do. My story is for His glory. I will remain consistent and accomplish everything He's instructed me to do, and I wish and hope the

Belief and Consistency

same for you! Whatever it is, *keep going!* Be consistent and watch the Father work in you, through you, and for you! You've got this, boo, because He has you! We're in this thang together. I know God is working it out for me in *His* timing. He's the Creator of time, and as long as I show up, He'll show up. Watch Him work!

Journey to the Authentic Me

CHAPTER 9

THE WAITING (PATIENCE)

Journey to the Authentic Me

Is anyone else having trouble with waiting, or is it just me? God revealed to me that I lack patience, and I see that heavily. Patience is all about endurance...it's all about being able to go through and wait well. It's not punishment. It's meant to slow us down from being so fast-paced and go, go, go, go. It's a means to teach us to trust in the One who's the keeper of our souls. But why is waiting so hard, though?! I wanted everything God promised me, like *yesterday*. That's the problem...we live in a right now culture... we want it now and gotta have it *now!* We want everything microwaved, fast, quick, and easy! Seems like everything I've been waiting for is at my fingertips but still outta my reach. And then, when I can almost see it, the enemy always tries to knock the wind out of me. My problem is letting him get to me, and then I get in my head and overthink everything. The one thing he always tries to make me think is that I'm alone in this waiting game, and the truth is, I'm never alone, even if I feel like I am.

Earlier, I briefly mentioned my desire for companionship. Sixteen-year-old me had my whole adulthood planned out (or so I thought). I just knew I was going to marry my then crush, and might I add that a crush is a terrible, *terrible* thing to

The Waiting (Patience)

have. I say that because you spend all this time liking someone, and you have no idea if your feelings are even reciprocated. I liked a dude for ten years. Ten years and he only saw me as a friend. I know, I know, *crazy*, right?! Nah, I was just loyal, I guess LOL. He and I grew up in the same church organization, and I just knew I was going to marry him LOL. But he didn't see me that way. He just saw me as the homie and a good support system. I eventually got over him, and I honestly didn't know what I was thinking! I was so zoned in on him that I didn't even know if the real thing was near! See how you can block your own blessings by being so hung up over someone or something?!

Back to sixteen-year-old me's plan...I envisioned being married by the age of twenty-four. I remember watching all my favorite TLC TV shows on Fridays because, as they used to say, "Friday is bride day!" Friday was when shows like *Say Yes to the Dress, Four Weddings,* and *I've Found the Gown* would come on, and I'm telling you...your girl was *obsessed!* I would faithfully watch those shows *every* single Friday in my later teenage years and early twenties, and my addiction to these shows was bad. I mean, it...was...bad! It got to the point where my mama was like, "Okay, girl. You ain't watching these shows no more." And it's not because the shows were bad or anything, because they weren't. It was actually about my heart. I didn't know this then, but I was idolizing marriage. Marriage isn't a bad thing. It's actually a good thing and a great desire to have because God is the One that places that desire in you. My problem was I used to dwell on it almost all the time, and it unknowingly became an idol in my heart, which is *not* okay. God really had to check me and knock down that hidden wall in my heart. He will not allow something, even if it's good, to take His throne and place in our hearts.

I know my man of God is on the way, and I know our marriage will be a Kingdom marriage for God's glory. It's been prophesied that the man of God and I will be like Aquila and Priscilla in the Bible, who opened the doors of their home for the people of God to come in and worship; we'll be in ministry together, which I think is so beautiful. I just have to keep myself encouraged.

I often experience what's called "seasonal depression" around holiday times when I feel overwhelmed and alone. It's crazy how time flies because in a year I'll be thirty, and some folks make it a habit of reminding me of that, especially when they make comments like, "You gettin' up there in age…when

The Waiting (Patience)

you gonna get married?" My response is always, "I don't know...whenever the Lord sends him is when." I don't even know why I let comments like this get to me, but I do (shaking my head at myself). But, the truth is, God told me the year that I'll get married, and I know He is the God of miracles because the man of God does not appear to be anywhere in sight. "Patience...patience, my child," God says. The wait is *not* punishment. There are some things God has to do and perfect in me before I can share my life with anyone else. I have to be intimate with God and seek after Him wholeheartedly *first,* and everything else will be added (Matthew 6:33). I have to learn to be content with just me and Jesus. I have to be okay with me, love me, and love God before I can give love to another. God is working on me, and He's working on him, too, before He brings us together.

When I think about patience and waiting, my mind immediately goes to the stories of Hannah and Samuel and Abraham and Sarah. In both stories, both women were waiting on motherhood; the only difference is one waited well while the other tried to take matters into her own hands. She (Sarah) was trying to be God, if you will. Hannah's story (1 Samuel 1) is that she shares her husband with another woman named Peninnah. Although Hannah was the woman he loved, she was barren while Peninnah was having all the kids. Peninnah wasn't gracious about it either; she mocked and picked at Hannah. Hannah could've chosen to bicker with Peninnah, but rather she chose to take her concerns to the One who could do something about her plight: her Heavenly Father. Hannah prayed and petitioned the Father for a child, and lo and behold, He did just that for her, and she dedicated her son, Samuel, to God, and he remained in the temple.

Abraham and Sarah were promised an heir. Their issue was belief because they were old in age. Sarah took matters into her own hands by giving Abraham her maid (Genesis 16), and her maid conceived a son named Ishmael. Ishmael was not the promised child, and then Sarah eventually regretted her decision because she began to despise her maid. Eventually, Sarah and Abraham conceived and had a son named Isaac, as God had promised. If they had waited without getting impatient or discouraged and looked through their spiritual eyes rather than their natural eyes, they would have seen five chapters down the line, their heir would be born (Genesis 21).

The Waiting (Patience)

This is encouragement for me because I'm waiting on purpose for purpose. Galatians 6:9 tells us not to be weary in well doing because if we faint not, we WILL reap a harvest. My marriage will be purposeful. My career will be purposeful. Although I love teaching my firsties (first graders), I know this is not my end. I know I won't be teaching all my life. God has shown me a glimpse of my future. I will sing, write, and minister full-time because God told me I had to be free to do it. The Lord told me to give Him a year. God wants me to walk out patience so I will have no choice but to trust Him and depend on Him, for He holds my life and future in His hands.

I let people's thoughts and opinions of me rule and get to me for the longest time. People *assume* because I have a couple of books out and music out that, I'm making that shmoney: *False!* And because they have these preconceptions in their heads, they'll ask for stuff and not believe me when I tell them I don't have it. Maybe they see something farther down the line I don't see at the moment? But they really be trippin' on me. The comments I get are ridiculous and really disheartening: "Anybody can get on iTunes or Apple Music. You not doing anything until you get on the radio;" "You been going to that church for six years and just now moving up? I bet the pastors don't even know your name;" "You need to go to your pastors and get them to endorse you. Nobody's gonna know who you are if you don't," just to list a few. I was even told I was wasting my time and money with these books and songs. I guess, in their minds, this is their way of telling me they feel my music should've taken off a long time ago? Deep, and I mean deep, down inside, I think they mean well? I don't know. But what I do know is that God is in control, and my books and songs will reach whom He wants them to reach.

If you're like me and in your season of waiting, be encouraged! I don't know what your wait is for...it could be a house, car, job, or something non-materialistic like healing for yourself or a loved one, the salvation of a loved one, a spouse, or even a child...be encouraged. God is *not* mocked (Galatians 6:7). In due season and time you WILL see the manifestation of what the Lord has promised. I'm reminded of Isaiah 40:31 and Psalm 27:14, which encourages us to wait on the Lord, and as we wait on Him, He *will* renew our strength and strengthen our hearts! We'll also mount up with wings as eagles and run and not be weary, walk, and not faint! I've said it before, and I'll say it again, the wait is NOT punishment!

The Waiting (Patience)

Think about your favorite slow-cooked meal. It may take a while for the flavors to marinate together and for everything to be well done, but the end result will be well worth it! It's going to be rewarding and worth all the time that you've invested!

God is slow cooking you! He's processing you. And believe me, processing doesn't feel good, but it's a *necessity*. During this time, God is purging and pruning you of everything that needs to come out. He peels back the layers of every hurt, pain, or wicked thing we try to hide from Him. We all know you *can't* hide anything from God. But God prunes us and heals us to get what needs to come out and what He desires to put in us (His Holy Spirit). Certain things you may have been waiting for, and certain things I've been waiting for, God has delayed because He wants us to be able to steward what He gives us well. He's such a good, good Father, and He wants to ensure what we're given is handled properly. I've found that God wants me to be able to handle what He's given me well *and* maintain my character. So, rather than dishing or handing His promises out right away, He chooses to process me because He knows I need it.

So, why does God want me...us to be patient? It's to slow us down from this fast-paced world and teach us how to depend on and trust in Him alone. So, here's a prayer for both of us:

God, teach us how to wait on You and not grow weary in doing so because we SHALL reap a harvest if we faint not. Teach us how to trust in You and depend on You. Help us to worship You while we wait. We thank You for the process and slow cooking in Jesus' name, amen.

Be encouraged in your wait, friends. *I love you,* and I'm cheering and rooting for you!

CHAPTER 10
PURITY

Journey to the Authentic Me

Purity has always been very important to me, and I always thought it was crazy that people made fun of me for it. Yes, I'm a twenty-nine-year-old virgin, and what about it? I will remain so until I am married. People especially thought I took it to the extreme whenever they would find out I hadn't had my first kiss or hadn't ever dated anyone yet. Not that it's any of their business, but when people ask me questions about my life, I do my best to give them the real: honesty. I remember being in the workplace, and I was talking to a colleague. I don't remember how we got on the topic of dating, but I mentioned to her that I'd never dated anyone, and I heard a voice that said, "WhO DoEs ThAt?!" (Insert the Spongebob meme here). I turned in the direction of the voice to see another colleague looking at me in disgust. And I remember thinking, "I do!" but I ain't say it because the enemy tried to make me feel ashamed in that moment.

I never understood why I got made fun of for staying true to my convictions and trying to do the right thing. Remember earlier I told you I was accused of being gay because I never had a boyfriend. "Oh, you must be gay since you've never had a boyfriend," "You like girls?" "Oh yeah, you're definitely gay," were some of the comments I'd get on

Purity

the regular, and they are far from the truth. Actually, now that I think about it, these accusations actually started in elementary school, all because I was trying to read the back of another girl's shorts LOL. I was a youngin' and ain't know no better, so I figured what others were saying was true: FALSE yet again! But anywho, doing my best to live as holy as I know how and keep my body pure has always been my goal. As I got older, I realized that purity isn't just about waiting to have sex until marriage. Purity has a lot to do with your heart and mind, too, because you can be pure with your outward man, but your inward man be filthy.

I was told that I'm a "rare breed" because of what people see from the outside trying to look in. I've also been called an angel because I don't partake in cursing or alcohol, to name a few. While that is one of the greatest compliments I've ever received, I want you all to know that I am human, and I've gone through temptation and am tempted just like anyone else is. Because I desired companionship and marriage so much, I often battled with lust, and I hated this about myself. My issue with lust wasn't necessarily about sex; it was just me having a heavy desire to date someone. I didn't do nothing crazy (praise the Lord), but this may have been why I crushed so hard on that ninja from my previous church...I confused lust for love. I thought that because I liked him so much and desired him so badly, surely, I must love him, right? WRONG. I was lusting after him for a long time and not even realizing what it was until God revealed it to me. Thank the good Lord for revelation! I had to pray really hard for my deliverance. The enemy always tried to make me think I'd burn in my flesh, but this is not so. Thankfully, with the help of the Lord through the Holy Spirit transforming me from the inside out, He set me free from this bondage. It's through the daily crucifixion of the flesh as the flesh and the Spirit are at war with each other.

Galatians 5:16-25 ESV says, "But I say, walk by the Spirit, and you will not gratify the desires of the flesh. For the desires of the flesh are against the Spirit, and the desires of the Spirit are against the flesh, for these are opposed to each other, to keep you from doing the things you want to do. But if you are led by the Spirit, you are not under the law. Now the works of the flesh are evident: sexual immorality, impurity, sensuality, idolatry, sorcery, enmity, strife, jealousy, fits of anger, rivalries, dissensions, divisions, envy, drunkenness, orgies, and things like these. I warn you, as I

Purity

warned you before, that those who do such things will not inherit the kingdom of God. But the fruit of the Spirit is love, joy, peace, patience, kindness, goodness, faithfulness, gentles, self-control; against such things there is no law. **And those who belong to Christ Jesus have crucified the flesh with its passions and desires.** If we live by the Spirit, let us also keep in step with the Spirit."

I die daily to keep my flesh under subjection to the Holy Spirit living within me. I constantly ask the Lord to purify my mind and my heart from any wicked thing known and unknown. #HeartChecks come from being intimate with the Father and being open and bare before Him. He can't heal what you hide. He already knows about it, and He already sees it, so you might as well be open and honest with Him and allow Him to come in and cleanse you from the inside out. Allow Him to cut you. It might hurt for the moment, but the end result will bring so much healing in the long run. Wow! Isn't it amazing to serve a God that heals as He cuts you?! He does everything with our hearts and best interest in mind, and I'm so glad He came chasing after me to knock down every single wall in my heart that was hindering me from growth!

Journey to the Authentic Me

It's very important to God that our hearts are pure. Matthew 5:8 NIV says, "Blessed are the pure in heart, for they will see God." I remember having a very bizarre dream in my late teens. In the dream, I was being robbed, but rather than get upset with my robbers and report them, I opted to minister to them. I don't remember everything I told them in the dream, but what rings loud to this day is this: "You don't have to be clean, but God wants you to be pure." What I take from this is you may have done some things and messed up in the past, which may have stained you, but God removes those stains. He's the One that cleanses you. He's the One that purifies you! And He does it with His blood, the blood of Jesus that makes us white as snow! He erased our stains (now I'm crying buckets) and paid a debt that we could never repay. We. Are. FORGIVEN! Made clean and whole!

Psalm 51:10 NIV is my constant prayer, and I pray the same for you. It reads, "Create in me a pure heart, O God, and renew a steadfast spirit within me." No matter what it is or what you've done, He's God enough to handle it and cleanse you from it! Beloved, turn to Him and be made whole. I love you, and God does too!

CHAPTER 11

HEALING AND FREEDOM

Writing this book has brought me so much healing. I didn't want to do it because of the memories I had to relive while writing it; reliving rejection, embarrassment, identity issues, and the fear of even putting this out. But even through the hurt and the pain from all the feelings and emotions, God is healing me. I used to think I didn't really have a story to tell. I didn't think I had anything to share. But that's all lies! I do have a story to share, and it's important. My story can help someone else. I've been freed to help free others.

With the help of the Lord, I can help other young women, and young people in general, who are going through an identity crisis of not knowing who they are in Christ. I can help them to take their muzzles off as I've learned (and still am learning) to take off mine. I can help them understand their words are important and need to be shared. Sharing is how we help to free others; sharing is how we help to free one another. My goal is to create a domino effect of generations being freed to live authentically. No more battling with low self-esteem, no more not knowing their worth and value, no more doubt, no more fear, no more shame, no more holding back, no more delay, and NO MORE HIDING! My prayer is that when it breaks and pops off in you, it breaks and pops off in your entire family, everyone connected to your bloodline, and everyone connected to you, period.

This has honestly been a process for me. Processing never feels good in the moment(s) you're going through it, but the end reward is always well worth it. During this time, God purges and prunes you of everything that needs to come out. He peels back the layers of every hurt, pain, or wicked thing in our hearts we try to hide (and we all know we can't hide anything from Him). He prunes us to heal us, but He can't heal what we try to hide. He does it so He can get what needs to come out of us and what He needs in us (His Holy Spirit penetrating all areas of our hearts).

Remember when I told you that God is slow cooking you? It might take what seems like an eternity, but the end result will be well worth it! It's going to be rewarding and well worth all your time and efforts. I'm NOT going to lie; it feels like I've been going through processing: the beating, crushing, purging, shaking, pruning, you name it for a *long* time... *but* God says, "That's how He gets the oil out." Oh, how I despised the process, but it's all working for my good, and I'm being freed from me, and the oil of the Lord is being released.

Journey to the Authentic Me

Let me tell you about your girl, though...your girl went through Permission Room (shout out to my amazing pastor Pastor Jackie) and did all the things to be free...but guess what I did...I allowed the enemy to bind me up in the very things I had been freed from. I know, I know, I'm shaking my head at myself too. It was like he had me in a cycle that, at the time, I didn't know how to be free from. I'd be free for some time, get bound up again, be free again, get bound up again, and the cycle continued until something broke. Something HAD to break because I couldn't continue on like that! It was a miserable thing to be bound up by fear, doubt, low self-esteem, and the opinions of man, among other things, over and over again! That's not what true freedom is, and I couldn't operate how the Father intended for me to like that. *True freedom* is *not* going back into the things that bound you up and held you back. *True freedom* is when you're able to be your authentic self without letting fear and doubt get to you. It's when you throw man's opinions out the window because as long as Daddy (God) is pleased, that's all that matters. Let me tell you something people are always gonna have something to say no matter what you do. But let me ask you this: whose words matter more...theirs or God's? I

Healing and Freedom

choose the latter. God's thoughts about me and what He says about me is what matters most! Why does it matter what other people think anyway?! Get your deliverance today!

I had to learn this for myself. I got tired of going through the cycle of freedom. I wanted TRUE FREEDOM! I wanted to be free all the time, NOT sometimey freedom! My good sis, SiQuena, who I mentioned earlier, said it was like I was standing and watching a Ferris Wheel go round and round with my head doing the circular motions until I got tired. And she said that when it popped off in me, it would pop in my younger sister Alyssa, and then in our whole entire family! I'm proud to say this is definitely happening! By me walking in complete and total freedom, that sparked something inside of my sweet sister, and she's being her authentic self as well, with no care or worry in the world! I've also seen it in my uncles, cousins, aunts, and in my family all around! My pastor ALWAYS says, "Free people, free people," and I'm living proof! Her authentic freedom freed me, and mine is freeing my family and others. My sister and I are generational curse breakers, and it's been prophesied that we are answered prayers...we're the answers to our family's problems.

Journey to the Authentic Me

You're the answer too! My prayer for you is that you'd allow God to truly heal and free you! I'm not talking about that cycle of freedom like I was going through. I want that TRUE FREEDOM for you. I want that real freedom for you. I want you to be free to be you. People are waiting on the real you to show up. People's freedom depends on you being authentically you...their lives depend on it. You're here on assignment. Wherever you go...whether it's to a restaurant, the mall, or wherever...you may think you're going there for one thing, but it's really God that sent you there because you're there on assignment. I repeat, you're here on assignment! There are specific people assigned to you that only you can reach and get through with the help of the Holy Spirit. I'm just trying to get you to see how crucial you being you is! YOU MATTER! God needs you to be you and operate in your full calling, anointing, and the power given by the Holy Spirit! The Bible says in Acts 1:8 NLT, "But you will receive power when the Holy Spirit comes upon you. And you will be my witnesses, telling people about me everywhere—in Jerusalem, throughout Judea, in Samaria, and to the ends of the earth." I need you. The world needs YOU! Operate in the power of the Holy Spirit.

Healing and Freedom

If you don't remember or hear anything else, hear this: YOU ARE FREE! You've been freed through the cross. Jesus gave His life so that you could have life. John 8:36 NLT reads, "So if the Son sets you free, you are truly free." God, we thank You for freedom!

God, I thank You for setting us free! Thank You, Lord, for the heart checks. Thank You for the purging, pruning, beating, and crushing, for that's how You get the oil out of us and Your desire for the oil to flow within us. Thank You for this new level of freedom. Free from worry, doubt, shame, fear, and people's opinions. What You say about us is all that matters, and as long as we're pleasing You, that's all that matters. I just thank You, Lord, for healing me, saving me, and freeing me from me! I thank You for my brothers and sisters reading this who are walking in their true freedom and in your truth. I love You, Lord, and I'm forever grateful. In Jesus' name, amen.

Journey to the Authentic Me

CHAPTER 12
THRIVING CONNECTIONS

Journey to the Authentic Me

God has allowed me to be a part of some pretty amazing groups at my church, and He's allowed me to meet some incredible godly people. In addition to completing the Permission Room mentorship program, I also joined my church's Thrive course, which helped me to see it's not by good deeds or works that we are saved, but we are saved by God's grace and mercy. Titus 3:5 NLT says, "He saved us, not because of the righteous things we had done, but because of His mercy. He washed away our sins, giving us a new birth and new life through the Holy Spirit." God told me when I first signed up for Thrive I was really going to thrive, and by His grace, I've been doing just that! I'll be taking the last part of the course and graduating really soon, and I'm super excited. I will hold on to everything I've learned throughout this journey and apply it daily. God has really broken my shell and allowed me to blossom, and I'm forever grateful!

I've also joined great serve teams at my church in which I'm fulfilling purpose by singing in the children's ministry and greeting fellow partners and newcomers as they walk through the church doors and giving them the biggest smiles and hugs. I get the honor and privilege to serve alongside some of the most amazing people. Friends have become family for sure!

My prayers of godly friendships and kingdom connections have been answered. God has sent me some amazing sisters to do life with. Sisters who will pray with me and for me. Sisters who will tell me the truth in love and hold me accountable for every instruction God has given me...this being one of them. Sisters I can pour into and who will pour into me as well. Sisters who constantly remind me I am not alone and will go to war with and for me. One of my absolute best friends happens to be my hair stylist. Where you know you can go to get your hair slayed and get a word at the same time? Where?! It's still mind-boggling how intentional our God is! God has also sent me some amazing brothers too. He's sent godly men, godly brothers, to show me how I deserve to be treated as a daughter of Christ our King. And I pray the same thing for you.

I pray God sends you kingdom relationships. Whatever that looks like for you...whether it be a spouse, sisterhood, or brotherhood. May the Lord send you godly people to do life with. People of God who see your potential and who will help call forth and unlock what's been hidden inside of you for God's glory. These are the kinds of people you need surrounding you and in your corner.

CHAPTER 13

WHAT'S NEXT?

God has shown me a glimpse of my future, and He's preparing me for it. I don't know how, and I don't know when...but I most certainly know who, and that's God! And I know because He showed me a glimpse of what it's going to look like, and because HE SAID IT, it's going to happen, and I'm going to be ready because He's getting me ready! I'm going to continue to thrive and shine for Jesus. I'm going after ALL God has for me, and I'm going to be all He says I'll be! I'll have all He says I'll have too!

What's next for me? Love, peace, continued happiness, and chasing after God and the things of Him. More writing, more books, more songs, and I don't know, maybe some merch or clothing items? Who knows, but God knows! More growth, being mentored, and ultimately mentoring others. Traveling the world, new experiences, making new memories, growing wiser and older. Cheers to me being free to be me and you being free to be you!

As one of my favorite songs says, "Hello peace, hello joy, hello love. Hello strength, hello hope it's a new horizon...Fear is not my future. You are." And God is just getting started with me! This is only the beginning. Thanks for coming on this journey to authentic freedom with me. I hope my story blessed you in some way and that it encouraged you to be your real, authentic self. Nobody does it or can do it like you. The better you is the real you! As my good sis Iman says, "No more runnin', no more hidin,'" I'm going to be me! Thank You, Lord, for freeing me from me and giving me permission to be myself. Daddy, I'm grateful. We're only going up from here. Love y'all.

XOXO,

Allison

Made in the USA
Columbia, SC
06 April 2024